North Cascades National

Park Travel Guide

An updated Guidebook to exploring Nature, Adventures
and Activities

Diane F. Rhodes

TABLE OF CONTENT

Introduction to North Cascades.

North Cascades National Park, also known as the "American Alps," offers a breathtaking view of untouched wilderness, craggy peaks, and pure, glacially fed lakes. This park is nestled in Washington and provides a sanctuary for nature's unfettered magnificence. Whether you're a seasoned hiker, a casual spectator, or a family seeking an amazing adventure, the North Cascades has something to offer everyone.

The park has more than 500,000 acres of federally protected wilderness, supporting diverse habitats from lush lowlands to rugged peaks. This diversified landscape features a variety of habitats, each with its own set of attractions and experiences. The park has more glaciers than any other park in the United States outside of Alaska, and they feed streams and rivers that sculpt the rocky landscape.

Visitors are met by seemingly endless landscapes, with jagged peaks piercing the sky and valleys descending into mysterious depths. The air is fresh and refreshing, with the aroma of pine and the whisper of wind blowing through ancient forests. This is a place where you can genuinely escape from the hustle and bustle of contemporary life and immerse yourself in the beauty and awe of nature.

The park's extensive wilderness entices explorers and adventurers. It's a retreat for people who prefer isolation and a playground for those who crave adventure. Trails lead to stunning views, secretive forested retreats, and peaceful lakes that reflect the sky. The more daring can attempt difficult backcountry routes, which provide seclusion and a true sense of wilderness.

For individuals who enjoy nature but prefer less demanding activities, there are numerous chances for leisurely hikes, picnics by alpine lakes, and photography of some of the most stunning panoramas in the United States. The ever-changing light and shadows cast on the mountains are a photographer's dream, varying with the hour and season.

North Cascades is also a haven for various species. It is home to black bears, mountain goats, marmots, and a diverse range of birds, including the magnificent bald eagle. The park's diversified habitats sustain unique and fascinating species that survive in protected settings. Visitors are frequently thrilled by the sight of a deer grazing in a meadow or the sound of an owl at dusk.

Because of the park's commitment to preservation and conservation, these creatures can live in peace. Many tourists regard the opportunity to witness these species in their native habitat as a rare and treasured experience, reminding us of our obligation to maintain and preserve these landscapes for future generations.

Preservation activities in the North Cascades are critical for maintaining biological equilibrium and protecting the area from external environmental stresses. The park is a leader in ecological research, providing important data for understanding climate change and its effects on glacial retreat, wildlife habitats, and forest health.

As visitors, we play an important role in these conservation initiatives. By following Leave No Trace principles, we ensure our investigations do not compromise the park's delicate ecosystems. This dedication to conservation ensures that the North Cascades remain a pristine environment for decades to come.

North Cascades National Park is more than a destination; it's an experience. The park offers a variety of educational programs that explore the region's natural and cultural history. Ranger-led tours, interpretive walks, and junior ranger programs are all intended to improve your awareness of the environment and its history. These events are a fantastic way for visitors of all ages to develop a deeper understanding of the natural world and learn about the need to maintain our planet's wild spaces.

Consider the numerous possibilities when planning your vacation to North Cascades National Park. Whether it's the excitement of an early morning hike, the tranquility of a sunset over Diablo Lake, or the thrill of finding a rare species in its native habitat, the park provides a meaningful connection to nature. It beckons you to explore its depths, challenges you to new heights, and rewards you with unforgettable experiences.

North Cascades National Park is a unique hideaway where nature's grandeur is fully displayed. It is a place where you may experience nature's power while reflecting on your place within it. We encourage you to experience the raw beauty and wild energy of one of America's most astounding natural wonders.

Understanding North Cascades.

North Cascades National Park, Washington State's crown jewel, exemplifies nature's raw, unadulterated splendor. This section explores the park's rich history, the unique aspects of its topography and climate, and the vast wilderness.

History and Significance

The history of the North Cascades is as ancient as the rock formations that soar abruptly to the sky. Humans have interacted with this region for over 10,000 years, with Native American tribes such as the Skagit, Swinomish, and Nooksack weaving their lives and cultures into the high mountain valleys. These indigenous people negotiated the difficult terrain, subsisted on the abundant natural resources, and held the country sacred.

European explorers arrived in the late 18th century, but the harsh and hostile terrain made widespread exploration and colonization difficult. It wasn't until the late nineteenth and early twentieth century that the area experienced an inflow of prospectors, miners, and, subsequently, explorers and conservationists. The park's formation in 1968 was a huge step forward for environmental conservation efforts in the United States, recognizing the importance of preserving this unique habitat for future generations.

Today, the park is important for more than only its historical and cultural significance; it is also a vital sanctuary for biodiversity and a living laboratory for scientific study and environmental education. It symbolizes the continual battle and cooperation between development, conservation, and indigenous rights.

Geography and Climate

North Cascades National Park is known for its stunning vistas, which include some of the steepest and most difficult mountain ranges in the continental United States. The park covers about 500,000 acres, with elevations varying from less than 1,000 feet near the park's borders to more than 9,000 feet at Mount Shuksan's summit. This wide elevation variation helps to support the park's different habitats, which range from rainy temperate rainforests to desert ponderosa pine landscapes.

The climate of the North Cascades is as diverse as its landscape. The western slopes receive plenty of rainfall, resulting in lush, dense forests and green alpine meadows. In contrast, the eastern slopes are under the mountain range's rain shadow, with substantially less precipitation, resulting in sparse, semi-arid conditions. This variation in climate conditions supports diverse flora and fauna, which adapt to niches created by nature's extremes.

Overview of the park.

North Cascades National Park has multiple sections with activities and experiences. The park is part of the larger North Cascades National Park Complex, including the National Recreation Areas at Ross Lake and Lake Chelan. These sections are more accessible and offer a variety of recreational possibilities, such as hiking, boating, and fishing, but the park itself is recognized for its difficult backcountry terrain.

The park's environment features rugged peaks, deep valleys, cascading waterfalls, and over 300 glaciers, the most of any park in the United States other than Alaska. These glaciers are important because they feed the rivers and lakes that dot the terrain, sustaining human and wildlife habitats. The vast path system allows tourists to experience high mountain passes, tranquil woodlands, and open meadows brimming with wildflowers.

The park's management focuses on protecting its natural beauty and ecological health. Efforts are focused on path maintenance, invasive species control, and scientific research to monitor and counteract the effects of climate change on the park's glaciers and biodiversity.

North Cascades National Park provides a remarkable trip through history, ecology, and the continuing spirit of conservation. Its rich history illustrates Indigenous peoples' tenacity and early explorers' pioneering zeal. Its diversified geography and climate provide habitat for various life, making it an important place for ecological research. This park is more than just a recreational area; it is also an important resource for environmental preservation and a symbol of the long-term worth of natural places in our world.

Planning Your Visit to North Cascades National Park.

North Cascades National Park offers an incredible tour through some of North America's most breathtaking vistas. To make the most of your vacation, you must first grasp the logistics, which include everything from the ideal times to visit to navigating entrance procedures and following park restrictions. Here's a thorough guide to help you plan efficiently.

Best Time to Visit

Spring (April-June): As the snow melts and wildflowers emerge at lower elevations, the North Cascades experience a new surge of life. Although many upper slopes may still be snow-covered, the lower trails provide excellent hiking options. This season also provides an opportunity to see the park's rebirth as rivers fill with snowmelt and wildlife emerges from winter hideouts.

Summer (July to September): is the most popular season for travelers due to the warm weather and easy access to high-altitude paths. This is the best time for hiking, camping, and fishing because practically all park facilities and roads are available. The park's alpine meadows are bursting with wildflowers, and the beautiful skies provide ideal photography and stargazing.

Autumn (October to Early November): As temperatures drop, the park's foliage transforms into stunning displays of autumn colors. As visitors decrease, the park's immense wildness becomes more solitary to explore. This season is also ideal for seeing wildlife as they prepare for the winter.

Winter (late November to March): The park is transformed into a snowy wonderland, perfect for snowshoeing, skiing, and snowboarding. However, access is limited because most roads and facilities were closed due to heavy snowfall. This season provides a serene, clean setting for individuals ready for cold-weather camping and hiking.

Visa and Travel Information

To enter the United States, international travelers must have a valid passport and, in most circumstances, a visa or an approved Electronic System for Travel Authorization (ESTA) under the Visa Waiver Program. You should consult the nearest U.S. Contact the Embassy or Consulate for further information and apply well before your travel dates.

To get to the North Cascades from the United States, most people fly into Seattle-Tacoma International Airport (SeaTac) and rent a car for the two-hour drive to the park. There are no direct public transportation connections to the park; therefore, having a vehicle is required to visit the different entrances and fully explore the region.

Park Entrance and Fees

North Cascades National Park has no entrance fees, making it one of the most accessible national parks in the country. However, some recreational activities and campgrounds within the park may charge fees, and parking at certain trailheads may require a Northwest Forest Pass.

The primary access points to the park are:

North Cascades Highway (State Route 20): This road runs across the park and provides access to several trailheads, visitor centers, and beautiful overlooks.

Hozomeen entry: Only accessible via a dirt road from Hope, British Columbia, this entry is less popular and provides more private access to the park's northern wilderness parts.

Cascade River Road: This road opens periodically and connects major hiking trails and climbing routes.

Park Rules and Safety Tips

Regulations:

Permits: Overnight backcountry expeditions require a permit, which can be obtained from visitor centers or scheduled online during high season.

Wildlife: Feeding wildlife is strictly prohibited since it disrupts natural behavior and can impair animal health.

Fires: Campfires are restricted to specific regions and situations; during dry spells, they may be altogether prohibited.

Drones: To avoid disturbing wildlife and visitors, drones are prohibited within the park's boundaries.

Safety Tips:

Prepare for the Weather: Weather in the Cascades can change quickly. Always pack waterproof gear and layers for warmth.

Stay on Designated pathways: To preserve the delicate environment and ensure your safety, stay on marked pathways.

Wildlife Encounters: Stay a safe distance from wildlife. If you encounter bears or other huge mammals, don't flee; carefully back away.

Emergency Preparedness: Mobile reception is spotty in most parts of the park. Bring a map, compass, and personal locator beacon when hiking distant routes.

By following these instructions and planning accordingly, your vacation to North Cascades National Park will be both fun and safe, allowing you to fully immerse yourself in the splendor of one of America's best natural environments.

Getting to North Cascades National Park.

North Cascades National Park, with its immense wildness and breathtaking natural beauty, welcomes tourists to explore the heart of the Pacific Northwest. Here's a comprehensive reference for planning your trip to this magnificent park, covering everything from directions and maps to nearby airports and local transit alternatives.

Directions and Maps

From Seattle:

To get to North Cascades National Park from Seattle, follow Interstate 5 north toward Burlington. Exit at State Route 20, also known as the North Cascades Highway. This picturesque route takes you directly into the park. Traveling from Seattle to the park headquarters in Sedro-Woolley takes around 1.5 hours and covers 70 miles.

From Vancouver, British Columbia:

For those arriving from Vancouver, use BC-99 S south until it crosses into the United States and becomes I-5 S. From there, take Exit 230 onto State Route 20 East in Burlington, Washington. The distance is approximately 130 miles and normally takes little more than two hours, depending on border traffic.

Maps are needed to navigate the park's vast expanse and varied terrain. Updated maps are available at the park's visitor centers or the National Park Service's website. These maps show comprehensive itineraries and point out important overlooks, trailheads, and recreational spots, ensuring a well-informed and safe tour of the park.

Nearby Airports

Seattle–Tacoma International Airport (SEA): Seattle-Tacoma International Airport, located approximately 120 miles west of North Cascades National Park, is the primary entrance for most visitors to the region. It has multiple internal and international flights daily and is served by major airlines, giving it an easy choice for visitors from abroad.

Bellingham International Airport(BLI): Bellingham International Airport, located around 70 miles northwest of the park, offers a closer but smaller alternative. It has fewer domestic flights but is less crowded, allowing faster departures and arrivals.

Pangborn Memorial Airport (EAT), Wenatchee: Another option is Pangborn Memorial Airport, located about 135 miles southeast of the park. It primarily serves regional aircraft and might be a convenient entrance point for travelers traveling from the south or east of the country.

Each of these airports offers automobile rental services, which are strongly recommended for getting to and from North Cascades National Park because there is no direct public transportation to the park.

Local Transportation Options

Car Rental: Renting a car is the most flexible and convenient method of visiting North Cascades National Park. Car rental services are available at all major airports, and they offer a variety of vehicles, from economy models to SUVs, ideal for the park's harsh terrain.

Shuttle services: During the peak tourist season, various local shuttle services depart from surrounding cities such as

Seattle and Bellingham. These shuttles mostly serve hikers and drop off at major trailheads throughout the park. While this option may limit your freedom compared to owning a personal vehicle, it is an ideal solution for planning long hikes that begin and conclude at different locations.

Public transportation: While direct public transportation options to the park are limited, the Skagit Transit system provides service up to Sedro-Woolley, where you can transfer to a taxi or a pre-arranged shuttle to enter the park. This technique involves some preparation but might be a cost-effective solution.

Taxis and Ride-Share Services: Taxis and ride-sharing services like Uber and Lyft are available in major communities around the park, including Burlington and Bellingham. These can be utilized for direct transfers to the park or to reach lodging and other amenities on the outskirts.

In essence, getting to North Cascades National Park requires planning and adventure. Whether you prefer to drive through the breathtaking scenery at your speed or take a combination of public transportation and taxis, the journey to North Cascades is as memorable as the destination. Each route and form of transportation provides a distinct view of the stunning Pacific Northwest, laying the groundwork for a spectacular trip to one of America's most beloved national parks.

Accommodations in North Cascades National Park

North Cascades National Park has many lodgings to fit any visitor's needs, from peaceful campsites buried in the heart of the wilderness to comfortable housing alternatives just outside the park. Whether you like the rugged appeal of camping beneath the stars or the comfort of a nice bed, our guide will help you locate the ideal spot to stay in North Cascades.

Camping at the park

Developed campgrounds:

North Cascades National Park has numerous constructed campgrounds with various amenities, including picnic tables, fire pits, flush toilets, and running water. Popular campgrounds such as Newhalem Creek, Goodell Creek, and Colonial Creek are popular with families and casual campers due to their accessibility and picturesque settings. These places are great for individuals who want to experience nature without giving up basic amenities.

Newhalem Creek Campground: Situated near the park's visitor center, this campground provides easy access to trails and educational activities. It's ideal for first-time tourists who want to see the area's natural splendor.

Goodell Creek Campground: Located along the Skagit River, this site is popular with groups and those interested in water sports such as kayaking and fishing.

Colonial Creek Campground: is an excellent alternative for hikers because it provides direct access to paths leading to breathtaking views and alpine lakes.

Reservations are recommended for these campgrounds, particularly during the high summer months, as they tend to fill up rapidly. You can reserve a place by using the National Park Service's reservation system.

Primitive campgrounds:

For a more remote experience, the park also has rustic campers accessible via dirt roads. These locations, such as Hozomeen Campground and Thunder Creek, do not have water or bathroom facilities, making them ideal for people seeking a more rugged and basic camping experience.

Nearby Lodging

Those who prefer not to camp can find hotel options near the park's entrances. These include rural cabins, charming bed & breakfasts, and fully equipped hotels.

Ross Lake Resort: This one-of-a-kind resort, accessible only by trekking or boat, features individual cabins floating on Ross Lake. It's ideal for those seeking to blend comfort and excitement.

North Cascades Lodge in Stehekin: Located at the extremity of Lake Chelan, this secluded lodge is accessible by ferry, foot, or plane and provides a serene vacation with spectacular lake views and pleasant amenities.

Local Hotels & Motels: Visitors to surrounding towns such as Marblemount and Concrete can find various lodging options, including hotels, motels, and inns, giving a pleasant base for exploring the park.

These lodgings frequently offer additional amenities such as guided tours, dining facilities, and equipment rentals, enriching your stay in the North Cascades.

Backcountry Camping Tips:

Backcountry camping in the North Cascades is an incredible option for adventurers to immerse themselves in the park's untamed splendor. Here are some guidelines for a safe and pleasurable experience:

Permits: A backcountry permit is necessary for any overnight stay in the wilderness areas. These can be bought from the park's visitor centers or reserved online.

Plan Ahead: Research the location you intend to visit. Understand the geography, weather patterns, and wildlife activities. Always notify someone of your travel plans and planned return.

Pack wisely: Bring only what you need, but ensure you have water, food, shelter, and a first-aid kit. Packing little will make your trip more enjoyable.

Leave No Trace: To preserve the park's natural beauty, follow the Leave No Trace principles. Pack out all trash, stay on authorized pathways, and store food in bear-proof containers.

Be Bear Aware: The North Cascades are home to black and grizzly bears. Store food and fragrant goods properly, and know what to do if you encounter a bear.

Camping and lodging in North Cascades National Park provide several opportunities to explore the park's breathtaking natural beauty and diverse wildlife. Whether you pick a luxury lodge or an isolated backcountry site, the park's accommodations may accommodate your preferred level of adventure and comfort, making your visit an unforgettable natural retreat.

Local Cuisine & Dining in North Cascades National Park

Exploring North Cascades National Park is more than simply a visual feast; it can also be a culinary excursion. The region serves a distinct blend of local cuisine representing the Pacific Northwest's rich cultural past and natural bounty. Whether you're eating at a local restaurant or taking a picnic to enjoy near a magnificent alpine lake, North Cascades offers a variety of dining options to suit all preferences.

Restaurants and Local Eats

Stehekin Pastry Company: The Stehekin Pastry Company, located in the secluded village of Stehekin and only reachable by boat, plane, or a long climb, is a pleasant surprise for visitors. This beautiful bakery is known for its freshly baked goodies, hearty breakfasts and lunches, and a variety of delicious pastries and sweets. It's the ideal place to eat fresh cinnamon buns or a slice of berry pie made using locally sourced ingredients.

Buffalo Run Restaurant: Buffalo Run Restaurant in Marblemount is popular with locals and visitors. This rustic cafe serves a broad menu that includes bison burgers and vegetarian options made with fresh, local ingredients. The restaurant's comfortable atmosphere and pleasant service make it a good choice for a full lunch after a day of exploring the park.

The Eatery at Ross Lake Resort: For guests staying or visiting Ross Lake, The Eatery at Ross Lake Resort provides an excellent dining experience with views of the surrounding mountains and water. The menu offers simple fare like sandwiches and salads, but the locally sourced-fish dishes are a must-try.

Goodell Creek Café: Goodell Creek Cafe near the park's main entrance is well-known for its welcoming ambiance and great comfort food-style meals. Whether you want a hearty breakfast to start the day or a filling dinner, this cafe serves delicious food with stunning views.

Local breweries and wineries: The North Cascades region also has several breweries and vineyards that serve local craft beverages. Visit Birdsview Brewing Company in Concrete or Challenger Ridge Vineyard and Cellars for a sample of local beers and wines, often prepared with distinctive local ingredients and a pleasant way to unwind after hiking.

What to pack for picnics

Picnicking in North Cascades National Park is a wonderful opportunity to connect with nature while eating delicious meals. Here's what to bring for a gorgeous picnic:

Portable Food:

Sandwiches: Pack various sandwiches with locally sourced bread and deli goods. Consider pairing smoked salmon with cream cheese on a bagel or classic turkey and cheese on whole grain.

Wraps and burritos are simple to prepare and fill and less likely to become soggy. Fill them with grilled veggies, quinoa, beans, and salsa.

Snacks: Fresh fruits and vegetables, such as apples, oranges, carrots, and celery sticks, are healthful, hydrating, and easy to pack.

Nuts and trail mix are excellent energy sources and make for a quick snack. Customize your trail mix by adding nuts, dried fruits, and a sprinkle of chocolate for a delicious touch.

Sweets:

Homemade Cookies or Brownies: Easy to travel and always a hit, sweets like cookies or brownies make for an excellent picnic supper.

Local Treats: To give your picnic a distinct local taste, include local specialties such as fruit jams or honey.

Beverages:

Water: Always carry lots of water to stay hydrated.

Local Handmade Beverages: Bring a thermos of locally roasted coffee or a bottle of handmade cider for a special picnic treat.

Essentials:

Cooler: A portable cooler will keep your food and drinks chilled.

Reusable Dishes and Utensils: Choose reusable goods to reduce waste.

Picnic Blanket: For maximum comfort, choose a lightweight, waterproof blanket.

Dining in North Cascades National Park can be as adventurous or as relaxed as you like. The park accommodates all dining choices, from local cafes serving full meals to calm picnic areas surrounded by nature's majesty, adding to your enjoyment of this spectacular natural hideaway.

Major Attractions and Landmarks in North Cascades National Park.

North Cascades National Park in Washington is a beautiful terrain with rugged peaks, lush forests, and stunning waterways. This huge park has a variety of attractions and sites that attract people from all over the world to discover its natural beauty. Here's a detailed look at some of the main attractions and landmarks that make North Cascades a must-see.

Diablo Lake

Diablo Lake is one of the park's most photographed sceneries, notable for its brilliant turquoise waters caused by glacial sediment refracting light. The lake can be reached by the Diablo Lake Trail, a somewhat easy climb that offers breathtaking views of the lake and surrounding mountains. Visitors can get a closer look by taking a boat trip with the local utility business that maintains the Diablo Dam. These excursions include information about the region's ecological and geological history and how the dam operates.

Ross Lake

Ross Lake is a 20-mile serpentine body of water across the park's northern section. It is a popular destination for kayaking, fishing, and canoeing. The surrounding trails provide hikers with panoramic views of the lake and its surrounding peaks. The Ross Lake Resort, located on the lake, offers unique accommodations in floating cabins, bringing excitement to any visit.

Cascade Pass

Cascade Pass is among the most accessible and enjoyable hikes in North Cascades National Park. The 3.7-mile trail to the pass provides stunning views of the park's rough environment, which includes jagged peaks and broad valleys. More experienced hikers can continue from the pass to additional trails that lead to secluded alpine lakes and spectacular landscapes.

North Cascades Highway (State Route 20)

This picturesque highway is the primary route through North Cascades National Park, giving visitors quick access to many park attractions. The route itself features multiple pullouts with amazing vistas. Notable stops along the roadway include the Washington Pass Overlook, which provides a breathtaking view of Liberty Bell Mountain, and the Gorge Creek Falls Overlook, where visitors may stretch their legs and admire the cascade.

Stehekin

Stehekin, a remote community in North Cascades National Park, is only accessible by boat, plane, or trekking. It serves as a trailhead and has multiple hotel options, a visitor center, and the renowned Stehekin Pastry Company. The Stehekin Valley, with its rural charm and lack of road connections to the outside world, is an ideal retreat from the rush and bustle of daily life.

Desolation Peak

Desolation Peak, known for its literary connection to Jack Kerouac, who worked as a fire lookout here for a summer, is one of the park's most hard and rewarding walks. The trail is steep and hard, but it provides hikers with breathtaking views of the surrounding peaks and lakes. The fire lookout remains an iconic monument, offering an insight into the solitary life of a fire watcher.

Colonial Creek Campground

Colonial Creek Campground, located on the banks of Diablo Lake, has easy access to water-based activities and trailheads. The campground is popular for families and outdoor enthusiasts interested in boating, fishing, hiking, and animal viewing.

The Skagit River

The Skagit River flows through the park and is renowned for its world-class fly fishing and breathtaking beauty. The river is also an important habitat for salmon, which feeds a colony of bald eagles. In the winter, guided trips are provided to see the eagles that come to eat the salmon, providing a unique wildlife viewing opportunity.

The Picket Range

The Picket Range contains some of North Cascades National Park's most rocky and demanding terrain. This lonely area is not for the faint of heart. Still, it provides amazing benefits in seclusion, stunning scenery, and a sense of accomplishment from navigating one of the park's most demanding sections.

Each site and landmark provides a unique perspective on North Cascades National Park's natural splendor and different ecosystems. From calm lakes and lonely villages to demanding peaks and picturesque roads, the North Cascades has something for everyone, making it an amazing location for nature lovers and adventure seekers.

Scenic drives and viewpoints in North Cascades National Park

North Cascades National Park, with its magnificent mountain ranges, lush forests, and dazzling alpine lakes, has some of the most breathtaking driving routes and views in the United States. These scenic roadways and deliberately selected viewpoints allow visitors to enjoy the park's spectacular splendor from the comfort of their cars or on short walks to panoramic panoramas. This book includes must-see drives and perspectives that capture the spectacular allure of the North Cascades.

North Cascades Highway (State Route 20)

The North Cascades Highway, also known as State Route 20, runs through North Cascades National Park and connects several of the park's most popular sites. This road provides an intriguing journey through various scenery, ranging from lush forests to dramatic mountain vistas. Important stops on this picturesque journey include:

Washington Pass Overlook: This highway's highest point provides a breathtaking view of Liberty Bell Mountain and the surrounding peaks. The overlook is accessible by a short, paved loop walk with amazing panoramic views. It's especially gorgeous in the fall when the larch trees turn golden.

Diablo Lake Overlook: This overlook, one of the park's most iconic views, provides visitors with a breathtaking picture of Diablo Lake's vibrant blue waters, framed by snow-capped peaks. The viewpoint also features interpretive plaques that explain the lake's glacial origins and function in generating hydroelectric power for the region.

Rainy Pass Picnic Area: Located near Rainy Pass, this area serves as a trailhead for various trails and is a great place to have a picnic with a view. The neighboring trails provide casual strolls and access to more difficult walks, such as the one-up Maple Pass.

Gorge Creek Falls: This location includes a stunning suspension bridge and a view of the flowing Gorge Creek

Falls. It's a great spot to photograph, especially in the spring when the water flow is at its highest.

Cascade River Road

This less-traveled road leads from Marblemount to the Cascade Pass trailhead, where one of the park's most popular walks begins. The road winds through old-growth forests, with frequent pull-offs offering views of towering peaks and, on occasion, wildlife. Highlights on Cascade River Road include:

Lookout Mountain Lookout: This viewpoint offers panoramic views of the Skagit River Valley, Mount Baker, and the North Cascades and is accessible via a short but strenuous trek. The ancient fire lookout at the top affords a unique view of the surrounding woods.

Doubtful Lake Viewpoint: As you approach Cascade Pass, a detour to Doubtful Lake provides a breathtaking view of the lake set against the backdrop of Sahale Mountain. The area is particularly well-known for its brilliant summer wildflowers, making it a favorite photography destination.

Mount Baker Scenic Byway

While not totally within the park, the Mt. Baker Scenic Byway (State Route 542) is a worthwhile side trip for people visiting the North Cascades. The byway connects to the Mt. Baker Ski Area and provides several views along the way, including:

Artist Point: Located at the end of the Mt. Baker Scenic Byway, Artist Point is one of the most stunning overlooks in the Pacific Northwest. It offers views of Mt. Shuksan and Mt. Baker. The area offers various easy walking trails that offer diverse views of the surrounding alpine landscape.

Heather Meadows Visitor Center: Situated near the ski slope, this visitor center is surrounded by hiking routes that provide breathtaking views of mountain meadows, rocky peaks, and pure lakes. The facility features educational displays about the area's natural history and geology.

Exploring North Cascades National Park's beautiful routes and vistas takes you through some of the most breathtaking landscapes in North America. Each route and viewpoint provides a unique perspective on the park's natural splendor, allowing visitors to explore the immense nature, from spectacular mountain panoramas to peaceful lake views. These drives and places are destinations in and of themselves, with each turn and trail providing a distinct view of the spectacular North Cascades.

Wildlife Watching at North Cascades National Park

North Cascades National Park, a biodiversity hotspot in the Pacific Northwest, provides wildlife enthusiasts with a wide range of species to see in their native settings. The park offers a variety of wildlife viewing opportunities, including stately beasts, elusive birds, and aquatic life. This extensive guide delves into the best sites, suggestions, and ethical methods for wildlife viewing in the park.

The abundance of wildlife in the North Cascades

Mammals: The park is home to around 75 animal species. Observers can see large mammals, including black bears, elk, and deer. Gray wolves and wolverines are more difficult to spot, requiring patience and a little luck. The park's diverse heights and ecosystems sustain various species, including mountain goats on rocky outcrops and marmots whistling in alpine meadows.

Birds: Birdwatchers can enjoy seeing over 200 bird species that call the park home or a stopover on their migration. The area is well-known for its bald eagle population, especially along the Skagit River, where they eat salmon. Other remarkable species are the peregrine falcon, harlequin ducks, and the rare spotted owl.

Aquatic species: Life abounds in the North Cascades' rivers and lakes. The Skagit and Stehekin Rivers provide opportunities to see salmon and trout, particularly during the spawning season. Beavers and river otters are typical sights around waterways, allowing entertaining glimpses into their playful activities.

Prime Wildlife Watching Locations

Stehekin Valley: This secluded area, accessible only by boat or plane, provides unique opportunities for animal observation in a quiet atmosphere. The valley's thick woodlands and open meadows are ideal for observing deer, black bears, and other birds.

Hozomeen Campground: This less-frequented region near the Canadian border is great for individuals who want to see wildlife away from the crowd. Moose and black bears are frequently seen in the area.

Cascade pass: Cascade Pass is a popular hiking trail providing excellent viewing opportunities for marmots, mountain goats, and the occasional black bear. Birdwatchers may also catch sight of high-altitude birds such as ptarmigans and Clark's nutcrackers.

Diablo lake: Diablo Lake's rich, glacially fed waters make it a hotspot for aquatic creatures and birds. The surrounding woods and cliffs provide nesting sites for ospreys and eagles, making it an ideal setting for bird photography.

Tips For Successful Wildlife Watching

Best times for viewing: The ideal periods for wildlife activity are early morning and late evening. Animals are more active during the colder portions of the day, especially in the summer.

Quiet Observations: Wildlife is easily disturbed by noise. Maintaining a peaceful disposition might boost your chances of watching animals in their natural habitat.

Use binoculars and telephoto lenses: To avoid disturbing wildlife, use binoculars or a camera with a telescopic lens to get close-up views. This ensures the safety of both the animals and the spectators, especially while monitoring predators or huge beasts.

Patience is key: Wildlife observing might take a lot of patience. Animals may not emerge when expected, so be prepared to wait quietly for extended periods.

Ethical Wildlife Watching.

Maintain a Safe Distance: Always maintain a safe and respectful distance from wildlife. This protects you and the animals and maintains the natural integrity of their behaviors and surroundings.

Do not feed the animals: Feeding wildlife can change their natural foraging activities and expose them to potentially dangerous foods. Always keep your munchies for yourself.

Stay on trails: Stay on authorized trails to ensure the safety of both wildlife and yourself. This helps to lessen human impact on natural habitats and reduces the likelihood of unexpected wildlife interactions.

Respect the environment: Make sure to leave no sign of your stay. Litter can harm wildlife and destroy the environment.

Wildlife watching in North Cascades National Park is a rewarding activity that connects you with nature's beauties. By following these recommendations and respecting the natural environment, you can enjoy seeing diverse animals while guaranteeing their survival for future generations. Whether you are an avid birdwatcher, a mammal fanatic, or a nature lover, the park's vast ecosystems provide several possibilities to engage with nature profoundly and respectfully.

Hiking Trails in North Cascades National Park

North Cascades National Park is a hiker's dream, with a vast network of trails catering to all levels of expertise and stamina. This park offers many possibilities, from easy, family-friendly pathways with spectacular views that require little effort to challenging wilderness excursions that test even the most experienced hiker. This thorough book explores the park's hiking opportunities, showcasing family-friendly trails, great day walks, and tough backpacking routes.

Easy trails for families.

Sterling Munro Trail:

Length: 0.5 kilometers roundtrip

Negligible elevation gain.

This short, totally accessible walk leads to a beautiful vista of the Picket Range. Beginning at the visitor center near Newhalem, this paved trail is ideal for families with young children or individuals with mobility issues. The vista at the conclusion is a wonderful introduction to the park's stunning scenery, making it a worthwhile visit for all ages.

Trail of Cedars:

Length: one-mile round trip

Negligible elevation gain.

The Trail of the Cedars is an easy circle that winds through ancient forests, passing by boardwalks and old-growth giants. This route, located near Newhalem, is not only accessible but also includes educational interpretive signs that explain the local ecology, making it ideal for families wishing to combine a relaxing walk with environmental education.

Happy Creek Forest Walk:

Distance: 1.8 miles round trip

Elevation gain: Little

The Happy Creek Forest Walk is ideal for exploring the North Cascades' rich undergrowth and vibrant ecosystems. The trail is gentle and well-maintained, flowing alongside Happy Creek and through lush forest. It allows children and adults to enjoy the peace of the park's woodlands without climbing steeply.

Day hikes

Blue Lake Trail:

Distance: 4.4 kilometers round trip

Elevation Gain: 1,050 feet

The Blue Lake Trail is a moderately demanding journey that rewards walkers with breathtaking views of a pristine alpine lake surrounded by steep peaks. The track, decked with wildflowers in late spring and summer, is well-marked and maintained, making it a popular destination for day walkers. Blue Lake's fresh, clear waters make for a peaceful place to rest and picnic before returning.

Maple Pass Loop:

Length: 7.2-mile loop

Elevation Gain: 2,000 feet

This circle hike is one of the most spectacular in the park, with panoramic vistas of the North Cascades. The trail climbs steadily to the ridge line, where hikers may see Lake Ann and the surrounding mountain ranges. Suitable for more ambitious families and day hikers, the Maple Pass Loop is especially beautiful when the larch trees turn a dazzling gold in the fall.

Cascade Pass Trail:

Length: 7 kilometers roundtrip

Elevation Gain: 1,800 feet

The Cascade Pass Trail is possibly the most popular day trek in the park. It offers stunning views for a moderate effort. The trail ascends through switchbacks to the pass, which offers panoramic views of glaciated valleys and peaks. For those with more energy, the trail continues to Sahale Arm, a more difficult extension that provides close-up views of Sahale Mountain and the hanging glaciers.

Challenging Backpacking Routes

Copper Ridge Loop:

Length: 34-mile loop

Elevation gain: variable.

The Copper Ridge Loop is challenging for experienced backpackers, but it rewards them with some of the park's most breathtaking views. This route takes many days to complete and covers a variety of terrain, including ridge lines with panoramic vistas and deep, forested valleys. Backpackers must be self-sufficient and prepared for sudden weather changes, making this route suited for seasoned travelers.

Devil's Dome Loop:

Length: 42.5 mile loop

Elevation Gain: High

Another high-commitment route, the Devil's Dome Loop, provides a tough backcountry adventure with major elevation changes and breathtaking Jack Mountain and Ross Lake vistas. The loop is known for its difficult climbs and descents, but it also provides hikers access to some of the park's most secluded and wild areas.

Ptarmigan Traverses:

Length: About 35 miles one way.

Elevation gain: extensive

The Ptarmigan Traverse is a challenging route that demands mountaineering ability and glacier navigation experience. This trail is more of an alpine route that traverses multiple glaciers than a well-designated path. It is usually performed over several days and necessitates meticulous preparation and navigation skills.

Whether you're a family looking for a stroll through ancient forests, a day hiker looking for panoramic views, or a backpacker ready to tackle some of the most difficult trails in the Pacific Northwest, North Cascades National Park has trails that promise unforgettable adventures and breathtaking natural beauty. Each trail offers a unique opportunity to experience the rough nature, interact with the local creatures, and discover the region's rich biodiversity.

Adventure Activities at North Cascades National Park.

North Cascades National Park, recognized for its rugged beauty and various landscapes, offers a variety of adventure activities suitable for thrill seekers and nature lovers. From ascending towering rock faces to skimming across beautiful rivers and slicing through new snow, the park offers a limitless variety of thrilling adventures. This book covers rock climbing, mountaineering, boating and fishing, and winter sports in North Cascades National Park.

Rock climbing and mountaineering

Rock Climbing:

The North Cascades are a refuge for rock climbers, with some of the most difficult and rewarding climbs in the Pacific Northwest. The park's granite spires and craggy cliffs offer climbers a wide range of routes, from beginner-friendly to experienced multi-pitch routes.

Liberty Bell Mountain: Liberty Bell is one of the park's most iconic climbing sites, with several classic routes, including the well-known Beckey Route. This climb is appropriate for intermediate to advanced climbers and offers spectacular views of the surrounding peaks.

Washington Pass: Located along the North Cascades Highway, Washington Pass offers a variety of climbing routes suitable for all skill levels. Popular climbs include South Early Winters Spire and Concord Tower, which have outstanding rock quality and stunning views.

Mount Shuksan's Southeast Ridge: offers an exciting alpine rock climbing experience for those looking to combine rock climbing and mountaineering. The route is notable for its solid granite and technical climbing sections, culminating in a beautiful peak.

Mountaineering:

The North Cascades are commonly referred to as the "American Alps," and with good cause. The park's glaciated peaks and inaccessible alpine environment provide some of the most difficult and rewarding mountaineering experiences in the United States.

Mount Baker: which stands at 10,781 feet, is a popular destination for climbers seeking glacier and alpine climbing experiences. The Coleman-Deming route is popular for first-time mountaineers since it offers a relatively easy ascent with breathtaking views of the North Cascades and Puget Sound.

Eldorado Peak: Known for its famous knife-edge ridge, Eldorado Peak is popular among skilled mountaineers. The climb entails traversing crevasses, steep snow slopes, and rock scrambling to reach one of the range's most stunning summits.

Forbidden Peak: provides traditional alpine climbing via its West Ridge route, regarded as one of North America's 50 classic climbs. The route includes rock climbing, snow travel, and technical ridge climbing, making it a difficult but rewarding ascent for experienced climbers.

Boating & Fishing

Boating:

North Cascades National Park has numerous lakes and rivers and is a boater's paradise. The park's pure waters provide chances for kayaking, canoeing, and motorboating, giving visitors a fresh view of the park's breathtaking scenery.

Ross Lake: One of the park's most popular boating sites, Ross Lake runs for 20 miles and provides a peaceful setting for paddling and motorboating. The lake's crystal-clear waters and surrounding peaks make it a beautiful place to explore. Ross Lake Resort rents canoes and kayaks and has many boat-in campsites for those who want to extend their journey.

Diablo Lake: Known for its beautiful blue waters, it is another great place to boat. Kayaking and canoeing are popular pastimes here, with numerous access spots and boat ramps. The lake's numerous islets and hidden coves offer limitless exploration options.

The Skagit River runs through the park and combines tranquil stretches with dramatic rapids, making it ideal for leisurely floats and adventurous white-water rafting trips. Guided rafting tours are provided, and they offer an exciting opportunity to explore the park's waterways.

Fishing:

North Cascades National Park has plenty to offer anglers, including robust fish populations and different fishing options. The park's lakes, rivers, and streams support a diverse range of animals, including trout, salmon, and char.

Ross Lake: This enormous reservoir is well-known for its superb fishing, which includes plentiful rainbow trout and kokanee salmon. Fishing from a boat or the shoreline can provide satisfying catches, and the gorgeous backdrop creates an outstanding fishing experience.

Diablo Lake: Diablo Lake, like Ross Lake, provides excellent fishing opportunities, particularly for rainbow and bull trout. The lake's excellent waters and attractive environment make it a popular fishing destination.

Skagit River: The Skagit River is noted for its salmon runs, especially in the fall when it teems with coho and chum salmon. The river also has strong steelhead and cutthroat trout concentrations, providing year-round fishing possibilities.

Winter sports

Skiing and snowboarding:

When winter blankets the North Cascades in snow, the park changes into a ski and snowboard playground. The location provides good chances for both backcountry skiing and resort-based sports.

Mount Baker Ski Area: Located just outside the park, it is known for its deep powder and steep terrain. The ski region receives some of North America's greatest snowfall totals, providing plenty of powder skiing and snowboarding options. It suits all ability levels, with groomed tracks and off-piste regions.

Backcountry Skiing: The park's extensive, unspoiled nature provides several backcountry skiing and splitboarding options. Popular sites include Mount Baker's slopes, the steep landscape near Washington Pass, and the Picket Range's secluded valleys. Skiers should be well-prepared and aware of avalanche safety, as the backcountry can be dangerous.

Snowshoeing and Cross-Country Skiing:

Snowshoeing and cross-country skiing are ideal for individuals who prefer a slower pace when exploring North Cascades National Park's winter landscape.

Rainy Pass has multiple trails suited for snowshoeing and cross-country skiing. The moderate topography and beautiful winter environment make it a popular destination for these activities.

Cascade River Road: When it snows, it turns into a winter paradise ideal for snowshoeing. The road is closed to automobiles during the winter, giving a calm and scenic approach through the park's icy forests and valleys.

Thunder Creek track: This track is open in the winter and provides a pretty easy route for snowshoers and cross-country skiers. The trail follows Thunder Creek, providing stunning views of the surrounding snow-covered peaks.

Winter mountaineering:

For those looking for the ultimate winter adventure, the North Cascades offer demanding winter mountaineering options. The park's glaciated peaks and harsh terrain make it an intimidating playground for expert climbers.

Mount Shuksan: Winter ascents of Mount Shuksan are serious undertakings that require considerable climbing abilities and experience. The climb requires crossing steep snow and ice slopes while dealing with possibly severe winter weather.

Eldorado Peak: Winter ascents of Eldorado Peak are as demanding, with the added challenge of heavy snow and treacherous weather. Climbers must prepare to be self-sufficient in difficult winter settings.

Boston Basin: This area has a variety of winter climbing routes, including the steep North Ridge of Forbidden Peak. The isolated and rugged character of the terrain means that only experienced and well-prepared climbers should attempt it.

Finally, North Cascades National Park is an adventurer's paradise with something for everyone. Whether you're conquering steep summits, kayaking across serene lakes, throwing a line in pristine waterways, or carving through fresh snow, the park's various landscapes and abundance of exploring options make for an amazing experience. Accept the challenge and immerse yourself in the natural splendor of North Cascades National Park.

Family-Friendly Activities at North Cascades National Park

Exploring North Cascades National Park with your family provides a unique opportunity to bond over stunning scenery and exciting activities. The park's diverse activities and pathways are precisely designed to pique the interest of young brains while also providing fun learning experiences for people of all ages. North Cascades is a perfect place for families wishing to expand their outdoor experience, with educational programs that deepen their awareness of nature and ranger-led tours that give a personal touch to their journey.

Educational Programs

North Cascades National Park offers a variety of educational activities that are both entertaining and informative, designed to pique the interest of both children and adults. These activities provide an excellent opportunity for your family to better understand the natural world and the value of environmental stewardship.

The Junior Ranger Program: is a delight for many of our younger visitors. It's an activity-based learning program in which youngsters complete a series of educational tasks to obtain a Junior Ranger badge. Wildlife spotting, plant identification, and learning about the park's ecological methods are among the activities available. This hands-on method educates, engages, and excites the children about being environmental defenders.

Nature programs: These programs cover specific themes such as geology, botany, and zoology. They are presented by knowledgeable park professionals and involve engaging discussions as well as practical demonstrations. They provide an opportunity for youngsters to ask questions and gain hands-on experience with scientific equipment, transforming abstract concepts into real teachings.

Storytelling Sessions: Storytelling is a timeless technique of learning that never fails to captivate. Park rangers tell stories about the park's history, indigenous cultures, and magnificent wildlife. These stories help children comprehend the area's rich background and the myths and legends that have shaped local traditions.

Kid-Friendly Trails

Hiking with children can be difficult, but North Cascades National Park has various trails suitable for small legs. These trails provide great views and opportunities to see wildlife.

Sterling Munro walk: Beginning near the Visitor Center, this short, half-mile walk is easily accessible and ideal for families with young children. The trail features interpretive markers describing the local ecosystem, making it a walking classroom for aspiring naturalists.

Trail of the Cedars: This slightly longer circle takes you through old woodlands along the Skagit River. The path is flat, with benches along the way where families can relax and enjoy the peaceful surroundings. Informational plaques reveal details on the old-growth forest and its inhabitants, making it both a learning experience and a physical activity.

Happy Creek Forest Walk: Ideal for families, this walk is slightly over a mile long and takes you through lush greenery and along streams with relaxing sounds of flowing water. It is a sensory delight for children, enabling them to utilize their senses to discover their surroundings.

Ranger-led tours

Ranger-led tours are among the greatest ways to experience North Cascades National Park. These excursions are supervised by knowledgeable park rangers who can personalize the experience to a family's interests and physical capabilities.

Family Discovery hikes: These short guided hikes explore the park's vegetation and fauna. Rangers teach students how to track animals, identify plants, and explain how each species fits into the ecology.

Nightly Campfire Programs: These gatherings occur in the park's campgrounds and include ranger talks, sing-alongs, and marshmallow roasting. It's a relaxing way for families to unwind after trekking while learning more about the park beneath the stars.

Wildlife Watching Tours: These are scheduled for the early mornings or late afternoons when wildlife is most active. Rangers lead families through prime wildlife habitats, using spotting scopes to allow even little visitors to see distant creatures.

North Cascades National Park offers a variety of activities ideal for families looking for educational and recreational options. The park is a playground of knowledge and adventure, offering hands-on learning in educational programs, mild treks along kid-friendly paths, and informative ranger-led tours. Participating in these family-friendly activities can give you and your children a deeper appreciation of the natural world and lifelong memories.

Shopping at North Cascades National Park: A Guide for Enthusiasts and Families

Shopping at North Cascades National Park provides a unique experience that differs from the typical retail therapy in cities. Within this beautiful wonderland, the retail options reflect the region's rich cultural tradition and magnificent natural beauty. This guide will visit local stores, visitor centers, and surrounding town markets to provide an exciting shopping experience that compliments the park's scenic charms.

Visitor Center Gift Shops

North Cascades National Park visitor centers are information hubs and collections of one-of-a-kind souvenirs and educational resources. These gift shops are great for collecting souvenirs that capture the essence of your trip.

The North Cascades National Park Visitor Center: located in Newhalem, sells various items, including books and maps on the park's flora, animals, geology, and unique crafts created by local craftsmen. Purchasing here benefits the park's maintenance and educational activities, providing a meaningful layer to each transaction.

Golden West Visitor Center: Located in Stehekin, this modest boutique offers a cozy and personalized shopping experience. It sells items unique to the Stehekin area and the upper reaches of Lake Chelan, such as handcrafted goods and locally created foods suitable for picnics or gifts.

Local Artisans and Craft Markets

Beyond the visitor centers, the communities surrounding North Cascades National Park are thriving with local artisans whose creations embody the essence of the Pacific Northwest.

Stehekin Artisan Market: is a seasonal marketplace that sells handcrafted goods such as ceramics, jewelry, woven baskets, and homemade skincare products. Each item recounts the tale of the region's natural and cultural heritage.

Newhalem Creek Crafts: is a local artist cooperative specializing in textiles and woodworking. Visitors can find wonderfully produced quilts, carved wooden ornaments, and handcrafted furniture, all reflecting the natural beauty and workmanship of the Cascades.

Specialty stores and boutiques

Several boutiques and specialty shops offer North Cascades-specific products for those wishing to sample local flavors and specialties.

Cascade Harvest: is a shop that focuses on locally sourced delicacies such as wild berries, handcrafted jams, and artisanal cheese. It's an excellent spot to discover the flavors of the Cascades, whether you're seeking a treat for yourself or gifts to take home.

Mountain Style Sports: This shop caters to outdoor enthusiasts, offering high-quality gear designed to withstand the rigorous demands of mountain expeditions. From hiking boots and backpacks to specialized climbing equipment, each piece is carefully chosen for its durability and appropriateness to the park's difficult terrain.

Nearby Town Markets

While North Cascades's surroundings offer delightful small-scale shops, other towns offer more diverse possibilities for visitors.

Sedro-Woolley Farmers Market: Just a short drive from the park, this bustling farmers market exhibits the region's agricultural riches. Visitors can enjoy a wide variety of fresh fruit, local meats, artisanal baked items, live music, and craft booths.

Burlington Antique Mall: For those who enjoy antiques and vintage finds, Burlington has a big antique mall with diverse products, including rustic farm implements and vintage Northwest art. It's a lovely site for people wishing to take some history home.

Shopping in and around North Cascades National Park complements the park's natural excursions and adventures. Whether looking for authentic artisan goods, local culinary pleasures, or unique outdoor gear, the region has many shopping options to suit all tastes and inclinations. Each purchase provides a concrete reminder of your visit, benefits the local economy, and helps upkeep this lovely park. While exploring the rocky terrain, take advantage of the unique and intriguing shopping opportunities available to bring a piece of the North Cascades home.

Cultural Heritage of the North Cascades National Park

North Cascades National Park is both a breathtaking natural landscape and a culturally rich location. The park's history is inextricably linked to the lives of the indigenous peoples who have lived here for thousands of years and the explorers, settlers, and environmentalists who came after them. This guide delves into the park's indigenous history and historic landmarks, giving readers a thorough grasp of the area's cultural significance.

Indigenous History

For millennia, several Native American groups have lived on the territory that is now North Cascades National Park. These indigenous peoples, which include the Skagit, Swinomish, Sauk-Suiattle, and Nooksack tribes, have strong ties to the land, as seen by their diverse cultural traditions and historical history.

Early inhabitants: Archaeological evidence suggests that indigenous peoples have lived in the North Cascades region for over 9,000 years. These early inhabitants were hunter-gatherers who subsisted on the area's natural resources. They hunted deer and elk, fished rivers and lakes for salmon and trout, and collected various plant materials for food, medicine, and crafts.

Cultural Practices and Traditions: The indigenous tribes of the North Cascades formed a deep spiritual bond with the earth, reflected in their cultural rituals and customs. They revered the mountains, rivers, and forests, seeing them as sacred places inhabited by powerful spirits. This spiritual connection inspired their sustainable practices and respectful use of natural resources, safeguarding the land's abundance for future generations.

Trade and interaction: The North Cascades provided an important route for trade and interaction among diverse tribes. The tribes maintained vast trading networks, exchanging fish, game, herbs, and handcrafted objects like baskets and tools. They also shared knowledge and cultural practices, resulting in a diverse network of interrelated communities throughout the region.

European Contact and Impact: The entrance of European explorers and settlers in the late 18th and early 19th centuries caused considerable changes in the indigenous way of life. The introduction of new goods, technologies, and diseases had a significant impact on Native American communities. Despite these hurdles, the tribes adapted and maintained their cultural customs and ties to the land.

Modern Day Presence: Today, the descendants of these indigenous tribes live in the region and actively endeavor to maintain their traditional legacy. They work to safeguard holy sites, renew traditional traditions, and educate the public about their history and continued relationship with the North Cascades.

Historic sites in the park.

North Cascades National Park has several historic sites that provide insight into the region's rich cultural and historical past. These places tell the many stories of the individuals who have lived, worked, and traveled through the North Cascades over the centuries.

Skagit River Hydroelectric Project: The Skagit River Hydroelectric Project is one of the park's most significant historic sites. Built in the early twentieth century, this project has three dams—Diablo, Gorge, and Ross—that generate hydroelectric electricity for the Seattle metropolitan region. The construction of these dams significantly impacted the region's geography and development.

Diablo Dam: completed in 1930, was previously the world's tallest dam. The dam formed Diablo Lake, a reservoir with a remarkable blue color due to glacial silt. The neighboring visitor center allows visitors to explore the area while learning about the dam's history and impact.

Ross Dam: Built between 1937 and 1953, Ross Dam formed Ross Lake, another important reservoir in the hydroelectric complex. The Ross Lake Resort on the lake offers visitors a unique opportunity to stay in floating cabins while exploring the surrounding wilderness.

Stehekin Valley:

The Stehekin Valley, accessible only by boat, plane, or trekking, is a remote and historically significant park region.

The valley has been inhabited for thousands of years and was an important travel and commerce route for ancient peoples. Today, it remains a cultural and historical hotspot.

Buckner Homestead Historic District: This historic district comprises the Buckner Orchard and Homestead, founded in the late nineteenth century by early European settlers. The orchard, which still produces apples, is a testimony to historical agricultural traditions and offers an insight into the homesteaders' lives.

The Golden West Visitor Center: located near Stehekin, features displays of the valley's natural and cultural history. Visitors can learn about indigenous history, early settlers, and the region's evolution.

Newhalem:

Newhalem, a small village near the park's entrance, is a gateway to the North Cascades. The community has a rich history, including the Skagit River Hydroelectric Project and the Seattle City Light Corporation.

Trail of the Cedars: This easy trail in Newhalem takes visitors through a lovely forest of ancient cedar trees.

Interpretive plaques along the trail explain the area's natural and cultural heritage.

The historic Newhalem Depot, now part of the visitor center, was formerly a major transit hub for the hydroelectric project's development. The depot provides insight into the engineering and logistics issues encountered during the project's development.

Indigenous Culture Sites:

While many Indigenous cultural sites inside the park are not open to the public to conserve their holiness and integrity, some locations allow visitors to learn about Indigenous history and culture.

Ethnobotanical Garden: The North Cascades Institute's Environmental Learning Center houses an ethnobotanical garden displaying plants used by indigenous peoples for food, medicine, and craft. Interpretive signs provide information about the plants' traditional usage and cultural significance.

Cultural Programs and Events: The park and its partners organize cultural programs and events throughout the year, including storytelling, traditional crafts, and educational workshops to celebrate indigenous traditions. These programs allow visitors to learn directly from tribe members, gaining a better grasp of the region's traditional legacy.

North Cascades National Park's cultural heritage is a rich and intricate fabric of indigenous history and the stories of individuals who have lived and worked there for millennia. Visitors can better understand the cultural significance of this breathtaking natural area by seeing these ancient places and learning about the indigenous peoples who have lived here. Whether you are interested in the architectural wonders of the Skagit River Hydroelectric Project or the continuing traditions of indigenous cultures, North Cascades National Park provides several possibilities for cultural study and discovery.

Visitor Services in North Cascades National Park

North Cascades National Park provides various visitor services to enhance your experience and deepen your understanding of this breathtaking environment. From informative visitor centers and entertaining guided tours to accessible features and environmental stewardship efforts, the park strives to provide useful resources and experiences to all visitors.

Visitor Centers and Exhibitions

North Cascades Visitor Centre: The North Cascades Visitor Center, located near the hamlet of Newhalem, is a main source of information for visitors to the park. The center includes interactive exhibits about the park's geology, flora and animals, and cultural history. Highlights include:

Interactive Exhibits: These exhibits offer a detailed look at the park's ecosystems, fauna, and conservation initiatives. Visitors can learn about the causes that formed the spectacular landscapes and the numerous animals that live there.

Educational Films: The visitor center shows a range of educational films about the park's natural beauty and history. These films are played frequently and are a good introduction to the park.

Information Desk: Rangers are ready to answer inquiries, provide maps, and advise on hiking paths, camping areas, and other activities.

Golden West Visitor Centre: The Golden West Visitor Center provides a unique viewpoint on the park's cultural and environmental history in the isolated Stehekin Valley. It is only accessible by boat, plane, or hiking and offers a wealth of information on the valley and its inhabitants.

Historical displays: The center houses displays about the area's indigenous heritage, early European settlement, and the development of the Stehekin Valley.

Natural History Displays: Detailed displays and interactive exhibits help visitors learn about the valley's varied plant and animal life.

Ranger Programs: The Golden West Visitor Center provides frequent ranger-led programs and activities, such as guided walks and educational talks.

Skagit Info Center:

This facility, located near Marblemount, acts as the park's entrance and offers visitors the necessary information.

Trail Information: The center provides thorough information about trail conditions, weather forecasts, and backcountry permits.

Cultural exhibits reflect the Skagit River Hydroelectric Project's history and regional impact.

Guided Tours and Programs

Ranger-led Tours: Ranger-led tours are a fantastic way to see the park and learn from professional instructors. These trips cover many topics, including geology, wildlife, and cultural history.

Nature tours are short, instructive tours around the park's various ecosystems. They are suitable for all ages and offer an opportunity to learn about the region's flora and animals.

Historical Tours: These tours focus on the park's human history, including indigenous cultures and the construction of the Skagit River Hydroelectric Project.

Education Programs:

The park provides a variety of educational events to engage visitors of all ages.

The Junior Ranger Program is aimed at children and encourages them to learn about the park through engaging activities and games. By completing instructional activities, participants can obtain a Junior Ranger badge.

Workshops and Seminars: Throughout the year, the park offers workshops and seminars on various themes, including photography, birdwatching, and wilderness survival. Specialists guide these seminars and offer extensive knowledge and hands-on experience.

Boat tours:

Boat cruises on Ross Lake and Diablo Lake offer visitors a unique view of the park's landscapes.

Ross Lake Boat trips: Operated by the Ross Lake Resort, these trips provide a beautiful journey across the lake's breathtaking surroundings and the opportunity to learn about the region's natural and cultural history.

Diablo Lake Boat Tours: Seattle City Light provides in-depth tours of the Skagit River Hydroelectric Project and its regional influence.

Accessibility Features:

North Cascades National Park strives to make its natural wonders accessible to all tourists. The park has included a variety of amenities to accommodate those with impairments and provide an inclusive experience.

Accessible trails:

Several pathways in the park are intended to be accessible to people with mobility problems.

Sterling Munro Trail: This accessible trail leads to a beautiful view of the Picket Range. The paved route is wheelchair accessible and offers a spectacular view with no effort.

Trail of the Cedars: This easy circle trail has boardwalks and paved sections, making it accessible to all tourists. Interpretive signs along the trail provide information about the park's natural history.

Visitor centers:

All of the park's major tourist centers have accessibility facilities such as ramps, accessible restrooms, and designated parking areas.

Assistive devices: The park provides assistive listening devices and other aids to guests with hearing difficulties so they may enjoy ranger programs and instructional videos.

Service animals: Service animals are welcome throughout the park. Visitors with assistance animals should be aware of potential hazards, such as wildlife and uneven terrain, and prepare accordingly.

Environmental Stewardship

North Cascades National Park is committed to maintaining its natural and cultural treasures via rigorous conservation efforts and responsible visitor conduct.

Conservation efforts: The park participates in several conservation programs to safeguard its unique habitats and the creatures that live within them.

Glacier Monitoring: Scientists continuously monitor the park's glaciers to observe changes and better understand the effects of climate change. This research is critical for anticipating future environmental changes and designing mitigation methods.

Wildlife Protection: Efforts to conserve the park's wildlife include habitat restoration projects, wildlife corridors, and monitoring programs to check the health and movements of animals such as gray wolves and grizzly bears.

Invasive Species Management: The park actively combats and eradicates invasive plant and animal species that endanger natural ecosystems. These initiatives include manual removal, biological control, and public education campaigns.

How To Leave No Trace:

Visitors play an important part in maintaining the park's natural beauty and ecological integrity. Adhering to the

Leave No Trace principle reduces human effects on the environment.

Plan and Prepare: Proper planning ensures your stay is safe and enjoyable while minimizing environmental effects. This includes inspecting trail conditions, packing appropriate equipment, and understanding park rules.

Travel and Camp on Durable Surfaces: Stay on established pathways and campsites to avoid soil erosion and conserve sensitive vegetation.

Dispose of Waste Properly: Remove all rubbish, including food scraps, and dispose of human waste in specified areas or according to backcountry guidelines.

Leave What You Find: Respect the park's natural and cultural resources by not damaging plants, animals, or historical relics.

Reduce the impact of campfires by cooking on a camp stove and avoiding starting fires near sensitive areas. Where fires are authorized, utilize designated fire rings and keep them modest.

Respect wildlife by observing it from a distance and without feeding it. Store food securely to avoid attracting wildlife to campsites.

Be considerate of other visitors: Keep noise to a minimum and respect others' isolation. Respect other hikers on routes and respect park etiquette.

Volunteer Opportunities:

Volunteering in North Cascades National Park is a fantastic opportunity to give back and help protect this magnificent place for future generations.

Trail Maintenance: Volunteers help maintain and improve the park's extensive trail network. Tasks include cleaning the brush, correcting erosion, and constructing new path segments.

Habitat Restoration: Volunteer projects aim to restore damaged habitats by planting native species, eliminating exotic plants, and repairing disturbed regions.

Volunteers track wildlife populations and activities, providing crucial data to the park's conservation efforts.

Volunteers enhance the park's educational activities by leading tours, assisting with school groups, and working in visitor centers.

North Cascades National Park offers a variety of visitor amenities to help you get the most out of your vacation and interact with this beautiful area. From informative visitor centers and engaging guided tours to accessible features and vigorous conservation projects, the park strives to provide an enjoyable and responsible visit for all. Visitors may help preserve this amazing area for future generations by practicing environmental care and participating in volunteer activities.

Explore the Surrounding Area: Nearby Attractions & Day Trips from North Cascades National Park.

While North Cascades National Park is a wonderful location, the surrounding area has many activities worth visiting. From beautiful tiny villages to picturesque byways and other natural treasures, these surrounding attractions offer ideal options for enriching day outings.

Explore the Surrounding Area

Mount Baker-Snoqualmie National Forest.

Mount Baker-Snoqualmie National Forest, located adjacent to North Cascades National Park, is a popular destination for outdoor enthusiasts. This vast forest includes hiking paths, scenic rivers, and various campgrounds. Highlights include:

Heather Meadows: This region near Mount Baker Ski has beautiful alpine views and is ideal for summer wildflower viewing and fall foliage.

Artist Point, located near the terminus of Mount Baker Highway, offers panoramic views of Mount Baker and Mount Shuksan. During the summer, it is accessible by automobile and has various hiking routes.

Nooksack Falls: A short drive from Glacier, Nooksack Falls is a stunning cascade that may be seen from a well-kept observation platform.

Skagit Valley:

The Skagit Valley, located west of the North Cascades, is known for its fertile farming and vivid tulip fields. The valley's main attractions are as follows:

Skagit Valley Tulip Festival: Held every April, this festival draws tourists worldwide to witness the beautiful fields of tulips blooming. The festival includes farm tours, art displays, and family activities.

La Conner: This picturesque waterfront town is famous for its attractive boutiques, art galleries, and restaurants. It's an ideal spot for a stroll while admiring the magnificent vistas of the Swinomish Channel.

Deception Pass State Park: located just a short drive from Skagit Valley, is one of Washington's most popular parks. It provides breathtaking vistas of the Deception Pass Bridge, miles of hiking paths, and boating, fishing, and wildlife-watching opportunities.

Bellingham:

Bellingham, roughly an hour's drive from the North Cascades, is a dynamic city with a thriving cultural scene and various outdoor activities.

Fairhaven Historic District: This quaint neighborhood is home to well-preserved Victorian buildings, one-of-a-kind boutiques, and delicious restaurants. It's an excellent spot to explore on foot.

Whatcom Falls Park: This urban park features stunning waterfalls, picturesque paths, and picnic spaces. It's a popular destination for both locals and visitors.

Western Washington University's campus features a significant outdoor sculpture collection with breathtaking views of Bellingham Bay and the San Juan Islands.

Day Trips from the North Cascades

San Juan Islands:

A visit to the San Juan Islands provides a welcome contrast to the rough mountains of the North Cascades. The islands, accessible by ferry from Anacortes, are well-known for their stunning beauty, attractive communities, and plentiful wildlife.

Friday Harbor: the main town on the San Juan Islands, is a thriving cluster of art galleries, shopping, and restaurants. The Whale Museum is a must-see for everyone interested in marine life.

Orcas Island: known as the "Gem of the San Juans," has breathtaking landscapes, including Moran State Park, which features hiking paths and panoramic views from Mount Constitution.

Whale Watching: The waters surrounding the San Juan Islands are among the best places in the world to observe orcas. Numerous travel providers offer whale-watching tours, allowing you to observe these majestic creatures up close.

Leavenworth:

Leavenworth, located in the Cascade Mountains, is a Bavarian-style community that provides a distinct cultural experience. The town is recognized for its themed architecture, festivals, and outdoor activities.

Wander through streets adorned with alpine buildings, visit local shops, and eat German-inspired food at one of the many restaurants and breweries.

Outdoor activities in the nearby area include hiking, mountain biking, and river rafting. In the winter, adjacent Stevens Pass offers excellent skiing and snowboarding.

Events: Leavenworth hosts various events throughout the year, including Oktoberfest, the Christmas Lighting Festival, and the Bavarian Icefest, which create a festive ambiance during any visit.

Whidbey Island:

Whidbey Island: a short drive and boat trip from the North Cascades, is well-known for its scenic splendor, historic landmarks, and lovely small communities.

Ebey's Landing National Historical Reserve: preserves the island's agricultural and cultural legacy while also providing scenic pathways with views of the coastline and neighboring fields.

Langley: This lovely town is home to art galleries, boutiques, and delicious restaurants. It's also an excellent location for whale watching and beachcombing.

Fort Casey State Park: offers breathtaking vistas of Puget Sound and historic defenses to explore. The park also has a stunning lighthouse and miles of hiking trails.

Methow Valley:

The Methow Valley, located east of the North Cascades, is a stunning area recognized for its outdoor leisure opportunities and thriving artistic scene.

Winthrop: This western-themed town serves as the entrance to the Methow Valley. It has unique shops, restaurants, and the Shafer Historical Museum, which provides insight into the region's past.

Outdoor Activities: The valley is a haven for outdoor enthusiasts, with activities including hiking, mountain biking, and horseback riding in the summer and cross-country skiing and snowshoeing in the winter.

Methow routes: The Methow Valley has one of North America's most extensive cross-country ski trail networks, with over 200 kilometers of groomed routes.

Exploring the surrounding sites and taking day trips from North Cascades National Park can significantly enhance your vacation to the area. Whether you prefer the calm of the San Juan Islands, the cultural appeal of Leavenworth, the visual splendor of Whidbey Island, or the outdoor activities of the Methow Valley, there is something for everyone within a short drive from the park. These local places provide a variety of experiences to match the natural beauties of the North Cascades, making your trip to the Pacific Northwest unforgettable.

Travel Tips & Essentials for North Cascades National Park

North Cascades National Park is a treasure trove of natural beauty and adventure, but arranging a visit takes careful consideration to ensure a safe and pleasurable trip. Here is some vital travel advice to make the most of your vacation to this gorgeous park, from understanding the weather to packing the right items and taking the ideal snap.

Weather and Clothing Recommendations

Understanding Weather:

The weather in North Cascades National Park varies greatly due to its different geography and elevations. The weather can change quickly, so be prepared for various scenarios.

Spring (April to June): brings melting snow and blossoming wildflowers to lower elevations, although many higher paths may still be snow-covered. Temperatures fluctuate between the mid-30s and mid-60s Fahrenheit (1-18°C), with regular rain.

Summer (July to September): is the most popular season for visitors, with temperatures ranging from the mid-50s to the upper 70s (13-26°C). However, higher elevations might remain chilly, and afternoon thunderstorms are probable.

Fall (October–November): Cooler temperatures range from the 30s to the 60s (1–16°C). The foliage becomes colorful, and the park receives fewer visitors, making exploring a peaceful time.

Winter (December–March): The park changes into a snowy wonderland. Lower elevations may be gentler, while higher elevations receive significant snowfall, and temperatures frequently drop below freezing.

Clothing recommendations:

Dressing appropriately for the weather is essential for both comfort and safety. Here are some ideas about what to wear and bring:

Layering: To adjust to changing weather, use a layering method. Begin with a moisture-wicking base layer, then add an insulating layer for warmth before finishing with a waterproof and windproof outer layer.

Footwear: Most routes require sturdy, waterproof hiking footwear, especially if they are muddy or snowy. Comfortable walking shoes are sufficient for casual hikes.

Sun protection: accessories include a hat, sunglasses, and sunscreen. In the cooler months, gloves and a warm cap are required.

Rain Gear: Always bring a waterproof jacket and pants, regardless of the season, because the weather can change unexpectedly.

Use a daypack to transport basics like water, snacks, extra clothing layers, and a first-aid kit.

Photography Tips

North Cascades National Park is a photographer's dream, with breathtaking mountains, serene lakes, diverse fauna, and brilliant wildflowers. Here are some suggestions to help you capture the beauty of the park:

Golden Hours: The finest times to photograph are just after sunrise and before dusk. The gentle, warm light intensifies the landscape's colors and casts spectacular shadows.

Experiment with different viewpoints to give your photographs more depth and appeal. Shoot from low angles to highlight foreground objects or lofty vantage points for panoramic views.

Rule of Thirds: Arrange your photos using the rule of thirds. Consider dividing your frame into nine equal portions using horizontal and vertical lines. Place important items along these lines or at their intersections to create a harmonious and interesting arrangement.

Include humans: Including humans in your images can add a sense of scale and make the landscapes more striking. Capture candid shots of other hikers enjoying the landscape.

Wildlife Photography: Shoot wildlife using a telephoto lens at a safe distance. Be patient and walk gently to prevent frightening animals. Early mornings and late afternoons are frequently the greatest times to see wildlife.

Stabilization: Use a tripod to ensure stability, particularly in low-light situations or for long-exposure photos of waterfalls and rivers.

Editing: Use post-processing software to modify your photos' exposure, contrast, and saturation. Don't overdo it; instead, seek to keep the scene's natural charm.

Checklist For Hikers

Whether going on a short trip or a multi-day trek, proper equipment and supplies are essential. Here's a complete checklist to make sure you're prepared:

Essential Gear:

Backpack: A comfortable and well-fitting backpack to transport all of your gear.

Even if you have a GPS, a map and compass are useful backups.

Water & Purification: Bring enough water for your trip and a water purification device (filter, tablets) in case you need to refresh from natural sources.

Food: Bring high-energy snacks such as nuts, dried fruit, energy bars, and meals if you're going for a longer hike.

First-Aid Kit: Include bandages, antiseptic wipes, pain remedies, blister treatment, and personal prescriptions.

A multi-tool or knife can be used for various tasks, including rope cutting and meal preparation.

Fire Starter: Place matches, a lighter, or a fire starter in a waterproof container.

Emergency Shelter: A lightweight tarp or emergency bivvy for unplanned overnight stays.

Headlamp or flashlight: Equipped with extra batteries for low-light navigation.

Sun protection includes sunscreen, SPF-containing lip balm, and a wide-brimmed hat.

Clothing:

Base layers include moisture-wicking and quick-drying shirts and bottoms.

Insulating Layers: A fleece or down jacket will provide warmth.

Outer Layers: A waterproof and windproof jacket and pants.

Socks: Use wool or synthetic socks to avoid blisters.

Hat and gloves: Depending on the season, these can provide sun protection or warmth.

Optional but recommended:

Trekking poles can help you stay stable and reduce strain on your legs.

Bug Repellent: Especially during the warmer months.

Camera: To photograph the breathtaking scenery and wildlife.

Notebook and Pen: For recording observations or keeping a notebook.

Before you go:

Inform Someone: Tell a friend or family member about your hiking plans, including the route and approximate return time.

Check Conditions: Confirm the current trail conditions, weather forecasts, and potential hazards.

Permits: Ensure you have the essential permits for overnight backcountry trips.

Preparing for a journey to North Cascades National Park entails more than simply packing your bags. Understanding the weather, dressing appropriately, and having the proper gear can allow you to enjoy the park safely and comfortably. Whether taking breathtaking photos or going on an adventurous hike, these ideas will help you make the most of your trip to this incredible natural beauty.

Concluding Your North Cascades National Park Trip

As your adventure in North Cascades National Park ends, it's time to reflect on the great experiences you've had and make sure you leave with memories to treasure. The end of your trip provides a time to tie up loose ends, enjoy the final moments, and prepare for your return to normal life. Here are some suggestions and activities to help you end your visit positively.

Reflecting on Your Journey.

Capturing memories: Before you leave, take a moment to capture the essence of your journey. Review your images and videos, and consider making a scrapbook or digital album. These visual souvenirs will allow you to experience the breathtaking scenery, unique fauna, and unforgettable moments long after you've gone home.

Journaling: Writing down your experiences might be a helpful approach to absorb and recall your journey. Think about the treks you took, the views you visited, and the people you met. Take note of any memorable occasions or challenges you conquered. Journaling can also be useful for planning future trips or sharing your adventures with friends and family.

Final explorations: If time allows, go for one last climb or explore a viewpoint you may have missed. The peacefulness of early morning or late afternoon might bring a fresh perspective and a peaceful conclusion to your experience. Popular short treks, such as the Trail of the Cedars or a visit to Diablo Lake Overlook, are ideal for a final tour.

Packing and preparing for departure.

Leave no trace: As you pack up your campground or hotel, follow the Leave No Trace rules. Double-check your surroundings for trash, including small items such as food wrappers or bottle tops. Waste should be properly disposed of and, if possible, recycled. If you've been to a wilderness campsite, make sure to leave it as pristine as you found it.

Gear Check: Before you leave, check your gear to ensure you haven't forgotten anything. Check your tent, sleeping bag, cooking supplies, and other gear. If you've rented stuff, confirm the return process and deadlines to prevent additional fees.

Souvenir shopping: Consider purchasing a few souvenirs to commemorate your trip. The park's visitor centers frequently stock local crafts, clothes, and publications. A map of the trails you trekked, a book about the park's flora and fauna, or a locally created piece of art can make excellent keepsakes.

Saying Goodbye To Nature

Gratitude for the experience: Take a moment to be grateful for the natural beauty and experiences you've had. Recognizing the influence of your journey, whether through meditation, a quiet period of introspection, or a final walk through a beloved area, can bring a sense of closure and fulfillment.

Supporting conservation: Consider donating to organizations dedicated to the conservation and upkeep of North Cascades National Park. Your contribution can help to preserve this beautiful scenery for future generations. Many parks have foundations or friend organizations committed to their support; even a small donation can impact them.

Staying connected to the North Cascades.

Share Your Experience: Share your experience via social media, blogs, or community discussions. Highlighting your adventure can encourage others to visit and enjoy the park. Sharing information, favorite hikes, and images might help future visitors plan their travels.

Planning future visits: North Cascades National Park offers something unique each season. As you wrap up your journey, think about returning in the future. Whether you want to visit the park in a different season, try new routes, or revisit old favorites, planning your next journey helps keep the spirit of exploration alive.

Staying informed: Follow North Cascades National Park on social media or sign up for emails to stay updated on park news, activities, and conservation efforts. Connecting can help you stay involved with the park and its ongoing story.

Returning Home.

Travel Safety: As you prepare to leave, ensure your travel preparations are finalized, and you have a safe ride home. Double-check your route, especially if you're going through isolated locations with limited services. Make sure your vehicle is in good condition, and plan for rest stops and refueling.

Reintegrating: Returning to normal life after a holiday can be difficult. Use the great energy and tranquility you gained from your time outdoors to ease back into your routine. Small modifications, such as engaging in frequent outdoor activities or implementing conservation practices, might assist in maintaining the spirit of your vacation.

Sharing with loved ones: Make time to share your experiences with friends and family. Whether it's a photo slideshow, a comprehensive account of your travels, or simply sharing a treasured souvenir, including your loved ones can make your vacation much more enjoyable.

Final Thoughts

Concluding your North Cascades National Park journey entails more than simply packing up and leaving. It's an opportunity to reflect on the natural beauty you've seen, to ensure that you leave the park in pristine shape, and to keep the spirit of your trip with you in your daily life. By documenting memories, supporting conservation efforts, and planning future visits, you may maintain your connection to this magnificent area long after you've left its paths.

North Cascades National Park has a distinct blend of rugged terrain, tranquil scenery, and a rich cultural past. As you bid farewell to this amazing site, take memories of your visit, a deeper appreciation for the natural environment, and a pledge to preserve it for future generations. Safe travels, and until next time, may the magnificence of the North Cascades inspire and support you.

Appendix

AllTrails: Offers detailed information on hiking trails in North Cascades National Park, including user reviews, trail difficulty, and GPS route tracking.

National Park Service App: Features interactive maps, tours, and up-to-date information on park amenities, closures, and events.

Star Walk: Ideal for stargazing in the park, this app helps identify stars, planets, and constellations.

Weather Live: Provides real-time weather updates and forecasts to help plan your activities in the park.

Offline Survival Manual: Contains practical information on outdoor survival techniques, useful for remote areas with no cell service.

Emergency Contacts

Park Emergency Services: 555-1234 (Available 24/7 for all emergencies within the park)

Nearest Hospital: Cascade Valley Hospital, Arlington, WA - 555-5678

Ranger Station: Newhalem Visitor Center - 555-8765

Wildlife Concerns: North Cascades Wildlife Management - 555-4321

Forest Fire Hotline: 555-9988

Travel Checklist

Navigation: Maps, compass, GPS device, and downloaded offline maps.

Clothing: Weather-appropriate attire, hiking boots, rain gear, and extra layers.

Camping Gear: Tent, sleeping bag, camp stove, and food supplies.

Safety Items: First aid kit, bear spray, whistle, multi-tool, and flashlight.

Hydration and Nutrition: Water bottles, water purification system, energy snacks, and meals.

Sun Protection: Sunglasses, sun hat, and sunscreen.

Miscellaneous: Camera, binoculars, insect repellent, and personal items.

Frequently Asked Questions (FAQs)

What is the best time of year to visit North Cascades National Park?

- The best time to visit is from late June to early October when the weather is most stable and all facilities and roads are open.

Are there any entry fees for the park?

- No, North Cascades National Park does not charge an entrance fee, making it accessible to all visitors.

Can I bring my pet to the park?

- Pets are allowed in North Cascades but must be kept on a leash no longer than six feet and are not allowed on most trails, in wilderness areas, or in buildings.

What are the top must-see attractions in the park?

- Diablo Lake Overlook, Ross Lake, and the trails around Cascade Pass are highly recommended for breathtaking views and experiences.

Are there ranger-led programs available?

- Yes, the park offers a variety of ranger-led programs during the summer months, including guided hikes, educational talks, and junior ranger activities for children.

Sample Itineraries

3-Day Itinerary

Day 1: Visit the North Cascades Visitor Center. Hike the Trail of the Cedars and explore Newhalem Creek.

Day 2: Drive to Diablo Lake Overlook for photos, then kayak on Diablo Lake.

Day 3: Hike the Blue Lake Trail or the Maple Pass Loop before departing.

5-Day Itinerary

Day 1-2: Follow the 3-Day itinerary.

Day 3: Spend a full day exploring the Stehekin area, including a visit to Rainbow Falls.

Day 4: Take a leisurely hike in the Hozomeen area, known for its stunning views and less crowded paths.

Day 5: Relax at Colonial Creek Campground, enjoy fishing, or take short walks around the lake.

7-Day Itinerary

Day 1-5: Follow the 5-Day itinerary.

Day 6: Explore the Ross Lake area, consider renting a canoe for a unique view of the park.

Day 7: Spend your final day visiting the educational programs at the visitor center, catching any missed sights, or revisiting favorite spots.

Made in United States
Troutdale, OR
05/08/2025

31167552R00066